PERMISSION TO SPEAK

Holy Boldness

a series of short narratives

J. Althea

JanInk

Nashville, TN

Cover Design: Scott Ventura, Integraphix, Inc.

Publishing Consultant: Sedrik Newbern, Newbern Consulting, LLC

Editor: Linda Shew Wolf, Network Publishing Partners, Inc.

Printed in the United States of America
First Edition: May 2023

ISBN Paperback: 979-8-218-21012-0
Library of Congress Control Number: 2023909265

All Scripture references in this book are to the King James
version found on www.biblegateway.com

To my parents, Roberta and Elder Monzell McFarland,

my siblings, my children, and my grandchildren

ABOUT THE COVER

The Cross where Jesus died is a place that should never be taken for granted. Its lasting symbol of humility still causes me to bow in my spirit and give thanks for the sacrifice made so long ago. This cross, is still "The Cross" but some people have chosen to lavish and embellish it with things of the carnal world, forgetting its relevance and its awesome purpose. Let us not forget the journey that daily gives us our own cross experience, and remember to not change anything about that old rugged cross where Jesus hung, bled, and died.

PRAYING

Lord, help my unbelief, and when I see your hand at work, help my praise elevate.

Lord, allow me to always remember to test the spirit by the Spirit, and if that is not of you, help me escape and go through. I'll need help from You.

So, God, I need thee each hour, each day, everywhere I go, and where you lead, I will follow. I believe You only!

Amen

MY MORE AMAZING MOMENTS
(Table of Contents)

PREFACE

The Book of Habakkuk 1:2-4 states:

> O Lord, how long shall I cry, and thou wilt not hear!
> Even cry out unto thee of violence, and thou wilt not
> save. Why does thou show me see iniquity, and cause
> me to behold grievance? For spoiling and violence are
> before me: and there are that raise up strife and
> contention. Therefore the law is slacked, and judgment
> doth never go forth: for the wicked doth compass about
> the righteous; therefore wrong judgment proceeded.

But praises to the fact that Habakkuk continues seeking the
answer and is told to write the vision and make it plain. In
other words no embellishment; no personal agenda; no ego
satisfaction; just God's truth and nothing else matters.

Those passages are a part of my "More Amazing Moments." I
have had a few that cause me to either ask or beg the question
as Habakkuk did for "how long"? I am grateful that trouble
does not last always – that God is truly watching, listening, and
keeping record and time of all that goes on in this world and in
the church. I am also aware that He never adjusts His position

1

or His Word to accommodate anything that is not like him; therefore He has not amended anything from Genesis to Revelation.

It is also not so amazing to realize that the one place or entity that should be aware of God's refusal or need to change (church) is the very place(God's house) that is indifferent to supporting God's original plan. Let me explain:

It is also not amazing or surprising that the Word written in II Timothy 3:1-8 stands true, mainly in the worship center. You can read it yourself and see if you agree! I choose not to be a part of those voices that easily speak to change God's creation; nor do I choose to discredit the manger birth as a simple event in history; and I certainly refuse to cause an evaporation of the Holy Spirit for the sake of one's personal agenda as if in the human form, one deems himself equal to the Master.

This is my call to write the vision and pray that men and women will read it and know that God is still on the throne. I want to point out that He is watching, waiting, and God is taking note of all transgressions and indignations toward His Word. Most of all, His eye is on the righteous who refuse to turn their backs on one who has done so much, especially in giving His son Jesus to save this dying world. I love Him enough that He is working within me to write these "More Amazing Moments" for all your amazing moments in Christ – past, present, and for tomorrow.

Blessings!

THE QUESTION?

We stood in the rain and talked.

We talked a while, fussed, laughed, cried, and talked again. When we were quiet, the rain could be heard, just flowing downward as if, like us, it had no place to go. Walking away at that point would have been a small gesture, providing little more than "action sometimes speaks louder than words." But he asked again, and we talked some more. I wanted to answer. I really wanted to say that I would be committed. I asked him, "How long will you wait?"

The answer to the question, "Do I love Him?" is yes! That much I am sure of, and I am certain that He loves me. No one comes into your life without making an impression. They may be there temporarily, or for an extended stay. Nobody comes forward to touch your heart without piercing your soul. Maybe a copy of that month's *American Medical Association Journal* had an article about the heart. I could really have used a good, helpful story at this time. Nevertheless, it was probably too late now. He needed an answer, and although I hesitated, I knew I must answer.

Hold everything for just one moment, press pause, whatever it takes – slow the tape. I was afraid. I am scared of rejection, I hate the word "no" as much as anyone else, and I do not like being alone. If something is supposed to be a certain way, that is what I expect it to be. I like attention, too! When people ignore me, I feel unwanted and unneeded. It destroys my ability to perform. There is the chance that this fear can be overcome, yet I still hesitated.

Why wasn't there a sign in the sky, a hand writing on the wall, a star over Nashville, something more than talk? Even the rain had stopped, and I depended on it for support. I did not mean to sound sarcastic, and certainly not ungrateful for having been asked. I only wanted to be sure.

I turned and asked, "May I have just a few minutes more"? He replied, "No! An answer is required, or I must go."

There is only one answer: Lord, I will go!

*   *   *   *   *   *   *   *

The story above was written in June of 1998. I heard God calling but I was so conflicted, confused, and not ready to move. It took three more years for me to actually complete my answer to begin this holy race in ministry. People who are called by God do hesitate, but hesitation can be detrimental (look at Jonah). Reluctancy to get up and get going may result in a delay of blessings; and refusal can result in sickness and/or death. God ain't playing!

Moses thought he was unable to fulfill God's call because he had a speech issue; Sarah said she was too old to have a child; Esther thought she might die if she went before the King. In each event even in your own life, it is important to remember that you are not alone. Deuteronomy 31:6 states:

> Be strong and of a good courage, fear not, nor be afraid of them: for the LORD thy God, he it is that doth go with thee; he will not fail thee, nor forsake thee.

Why is serving God to serve others a difficult undertaking? What skills does one need in order to survive each test? To whom does one turn for help in knowing that this is the will of God? Read I John 4 for the clue ... test the spirits. Choosing to follow Jesus by becoming a part of the five-fold ministry is an honorable vocation not to be taken lightly.

God is not impressed by those who pursue this matter without His permission. It will not end well. Remember that God is love and He does yet speak audibly as well as by the Spirit.

Know His voice, not your choice. Know His call or you may be subject to fall. One more thing, remember that when consulting people about your journey, know that they are merely flesh. Flesh crumbles, dries up, loses its ability to hold on, so please always do the following ...

Look to the hills from which cometh your help, knowing it is of God.

MINDGAMES

People have choices. Your mind is an identifiable asset with no true location when properly exercised or trained. Technically it is housed in the brain, your head is its residence, but for some reason, the mind goes on vacation too often without a destination. I want to have someone create a GPS for the mind just to locate it when crazy happens, or people take leave of their senses. If you are believer and a soldier of Jesus Christ, you are reminded to let this mind be within you that is in Christ Jesus. In other words, one must think as Jesus thinks, responds, reacts, and receives information, so others see the comforter and are safe.

Question: Are you concerned about your mind? Do you ever consider that your thoughts do not align with how Jesus would respond or react? (Philippians 2:5-15)

Let this mind be in you, which was also in Christ Jesus:
Who, being in the form of God, thought it not robbery to be equal with God:

But made himself of no reputation, and took upon him the form of a servant, and was made in the likeness of men:

And being found in fashion as a man, he humbled himself, and became obedient unto death, even the death of the cross.

Wherefore God also hath highly exalted him, and given him a name which is above every name:

That at the name of Jesus every knee should bow, of things in heaven, and things in earth, and things under the earth;

And that every tongue should confess that Jesus Christ is Lord, to the glory of God the Father.

Wherefore, my beloved, as ye have always obeyed, not as in my presence only, but now much more in my absence, work out your own salvation with fear and trembling.

For it is God which worketh in you both to will and to do of his good pleasure.

Do all things without murmurings and disputings:

That ye may be blameless and harmless, the sons of God, without rebuke, in the midst of a crooked and

> perverse nation, among whom ye shine as lights in the
> world

Each of us has an ignorance of Christ's desire for our existence. Either this is true, or we simply are ignoring the spirit within us that shows evidence of His glory through us. Is this fear, or the failure to exercise our faith? Do we distrust, or do we consider this to be a short in the circuit? This world still holds no evidence that God does not exist – however it is constantly finding gods that replace the creator of this world. Mister Marvin Gaye asked the question, "What's going on?"

This is a good place to consider Mark 8:36:

> What shall it profit a man, if he should gain the whole
> world, and lose his own soul?

The world is indeed a ball of confusion, but if there's still blood running warm in your veins, choose God! This world will fade away. Noah warned the people for a long time that rain was coming. Lot told his family that once they left Sodom and Gomorrah they must not look back. Job's wife suggested that Job curse his God and die, but he listened to God instead. We all have something to lose if we do not have kinship with our God. This is a new day, but God remains the same, and the result for not following the will of God is still destruction.

Listen, following Jesus is not the end of your life as you know it, but the beginning of life eternal. Learning to deny yourself is not the end of your choices, but it is an essential value to prove to yourself that you are not your own. Matthew 16:24 records Jesus saying:

> Then said Jesus unto his disciples, if anyone would come after me, let him deny himself and take up his cross and follow me.

Your things, your stuff, your drama, your momma (Oh my)! Simply put, this scripture compels us to let go of things that so easily detour our course – things that tear us away from hours, days, minutes, etc. rather than things that draw us and keep us close to the Master.

TAKE THE SURVEY

1. How often do you pray or talk to God each day?
2. Do you worship only with others, or do you also worship alone behind closed doors?
3. Is the Holy Spirit leading your worship or is it an outside force or other people?

4.   Do you believe your prayer and worship is
      received?

Following Jesus is a good plan, but all plans must be worked.
Faith must be worked. Work is energy expelled, designed to
help you lose worldly weight and enemy hate. Let's face it, the
prince of this world does not like defeat, and your ability to
consume less crazy and more praising is just the ticket for
defeat.

Remember the childhood story of The Three Billy Goats
Gruff? There was a bridge that stood between the three Billy
goats and a pasture of beautiful green grass. In order to get
across the bridge, they would each have to encounter the ugly,
hungry troll. The smallest Billy goat trotted across the bridge to
be stopped by the troll but convinced the ugly troll that he was
too small to enjoy as a meal, but his brother was bigger, and
the troll allowed him to pass over. The second Billy goat faced
the same challenge, but also convinced the troll to wait for the
biggest brother. Well, the biggest brother then approached the
bridge, encountered the troll, and used all his energy to scare
the troll away. Thus, he was able, by faith, to join the other
brothers safely on the other side of the bridge. We're all trying

to get to the other side of the bridge by whatever means shown us through God's Word.

So, shall we tackle and conquer these mind games, (that which the flesh initiates) by the Word of God, prayer, praise/worship, and faith? I will give you the proposed answers for questions in the survey section above should you choose to use them.

RESPONSES

1. Pray until your enemies flee. Pray sitting, walking, standing, lying down, on your knees, just pray!

2. Worship at all times, alone or with others, until you are free of sin weight. Sing songs of Zion to comfort you.

3. Make certain that when you praise it is because you personally are giving honor to God, that the Holy Spirit is controlling your honor to God, and that no human orchestrates or intimidates the atmosphere of worship.

4. Preying is earthly gain; praying is heavenly gain. Choose wisely!

Jesus has control of all mind games. Remember, the devil has played a few on Him and lost. Defeat is not something that the enemy can take, and so he returns over and over to try again. Satan told Jesus that He was going away for a season. Guess what: This is that season. Hunker down until the storm passes, then move into the light of Jesus and never look back!

ONE BROKEN PEW

Recently a church which had been standing for years removed many of the older pews for new and updated, more comfortable pews. The congregation had become savvier with the way it wanted to present itself as a church, and the older pews (though still able to stand and fulfill their role) were voted out to the local dump, or to whosoever had need of them. Many of the newer members had complained of splinters tearing their clothes and the seats being so hard that it was hard to concentrate during service, so the decision to go into debt and purchase new pews was inevitable.

There were a few pews they decided to keep just for the sake of filling space, reminiscing on the past {since the pews had family names on them), and because the finance team said so. These pews had been in this church a while and had held many of the current members relatives (some founding fathers). These pews had been in place for many Homecomings, Annual Days, community events, etc. If these pews could talk, they would tell the story themselves. They might discuss the day Sister So-and-So shouted her wig off, or Brother So-and-So walked on top of the pews from the back to the front of the church. Oh yeah, these pews could tell the story of the conversations that should never have been held in church.

When all of the work was complete and the congregation returned on Sunday to see the updated work and pews, one pew stood out as it sat in the very front with one certain family name attached. The question was asked, "Why was this pew chosen to remain and also, who placed it here?"

Others asked, "Why was this one pew with the splinters and the discoloration placed here in front? It's in the way." They felt it should have been cast aside because it didn't match up to the fabric of the new look in the church. It was even stated that none of the young members would ever sit there because their clothes cost too much to be ripped by splinters, and some saints stated that they just didn't like the pew.

"Throw it away, burn it!" they proclaimed.

Then what, pray tell, did the really seasoned saints say? What did the pastor say? Well, I'm glad you asked. This pew was an object that was intended to be in place and serve its purpose even though it was old, tattered and torn. Not long after all the commotion over this pew silenced. . . the pew broke. Some rejoiced! Some wondered what happened to something that seemed so solid. What happened?

It turns out that someone was secretly praying that it would fall. Someone was hoping that it would catch on fire, and a few others thought that through magic it would just disappear. Funny thing about a remnant that has withstood the test of time and pressure – it was built a certain way and constructed with the best materials of that day. It wasn't expedient to just toss it out.

The pew was sent to the local carpenter named Jesus. He looked the pew over on all sides, on top and on the bottom, when He noticed something fascinating engraved underneath. The message was faint with wear but still visible enough to read the scripture from Romans 8 which began:

> "There is therefore now no condemnation to them which are in Christ Jesus, who walk not after the flesh, but after the Spirit."

The carpenter said, "Yes, I remember that passage is one from my friend Apostle Paul and it is good to remember." He then began to repair the pew, and before the end of the day, the pew appeared new, never broken, never scarred.

Soon the pastor was called and given the news that this matter was resolved. When the pastor and some of the members arrived to retrieve this pew, it had a new tag attached that read:

> "Be kind and tenderhearted to one another, love one another, forgive each other for just as God forgave once, He'll do it again."

The pew was put back in its place for further use, and the church learned to appreciate all the rich history of the church because of one broken pew!

AMISS

There are words amiss that should never have passed the channels of voice.

There are feathers in the air that cannot return, yet time has proven that plucked efforts are pain, better abstained, difficult to reclaim.

Careful now that your words be unsecure or come back and nest next to you. Time, they say, heals the most uncommon claims, especially when the-answer is written on record and the truth stands strong ... and deceit is defeated!

That tongue however bleeds without a sign of stopping, a stain has been left that the innocent bear. But do not mock the rodent that runs to the trap. There the truth is swept ... where pages of figures tell the tale, yet only to the wise shall it be unveiled!

WE MUST BE CAREFULLY TAUGHT

Someone dear to me shared this thought, "We must be carefully taught!"

First, I pondered why this message seemed a little foggy. It's because at the time 1 couldn't see the Blessing.

Words are interesting values that we learn, hear, and use from birth to the grave ...

But when misused, words can cause a lot of pain.

People use words to express love or hate.

They can be distorted, even covered in paint (that's kind of funny) ...

We always, or not always, try to wisely choose where words go,

Yet they crumble and cause others to stumble, and ...

Hurt so badly, oh so badly.

O' that today we would be carefully taught! We are mentally attired with a shield that protects and guards.

Words are not really meant to make us distraught, so today, choose words of favor and respect.

I hope we remember whenever we speak to use words as valuable assets, not painful disregard.

MY PRAYER

The Bible clearly reads in Proverbs 18:22:

> "Whoso findeth a wife findeth a good thing, and
> obtaineth favour of the Lord."

Notice that this event was not placed in the hand of a woman, and I am sure that God had His reasons for that. Anyway, if there is a chance of helping the Lord out, I figure that must be through prayer. He never said don't pray for a man, just that the man who finds you finds a good thing. Well, here we are, gentlemen ... as fair as Esther; as sought-after as Mary; and as productive as Lydia. What are you waiting for?

This prayer was written because although I know God knows everything, maybe He took a break or went to sleep like Jesus on the boat, and just had not received the message that I have called. Now I know that's crazy, but I thought I would throw that out there. It also seems that sometimes God is a little like molasses ... slow, slow, slow!

Well, there's one more scenario – maybe the angels decided to use a new cheap app for directions to my house and simply got lost! (I really should go ahead and ask for forgiveness now for all this crazy talk.) God forgive me, and please accept this prayer and allow me a do-over this day. Amen!

Prayer Prelude ...

Okay, pray for me as I begin this conversation. God, before I chalk up a failed attempt at relationship #1120, I resolve to write this letter to Christ so that my eyes are open and I'm fully conscious of my thoughts. It seems that when I close my eyes and pray, I sometimes lose sight of those particulars that need to be stated. So, I'm taking a new approach to asking for what I need and want. Keep in mind that this is personal. It is strictly between God and me, but because sharing is learning, you're invited to pray with me.

Dear Lord,

With sincere gratitude I thank you for your wisdom, guidance, and love. I thank you for protecting me from the devil soldiers, and constantly reminding me that I belong to you. I bless your name for your word when you said (and I paraphrase) that he who finds a wife, findeth a good thing. So, God I'm here to serve notice that I am not lost. I'm right here. Not only am I right here but I'm ready, willing, and more than able to accept the man you send. If you believe I'm eligible, I will keep asking until you stand him up in front of me.

This is personal, God, and I thank you for the opportunities I have endured, but I know some didn't work because I strutted out there with my fancy prance and got hurt. What in the world was I thinking? I cannot do this without you, and yes, I admit that I am not all that, and certainly without you, I am nothing. All my hopes and dreams rest in you for the best outcome and answer to this prayer. My mother used to say, if you want something from God, be specific.

I pause to make my special request: Me-made, Me-proclaimed, with My stamp of approval. I desire your ever-loving continued watchful eye, your guiding hand, and your forgiving ways so that my desire shall be given and sent from on high. Lord, I am placing my order for a man who fears you, yet a man who loves you. I ask for a man with complete capacities for my personal needs; a high 5- or 6-figure salary for our needs; a love of family for my protective needs; 5'8-6'0, not fat, not skinny (booty right and tight); easy on the eyes whether asleep or awake.

Now Lord, I'll tell you what I don't like. I abhor a liar – can't stand 'em. I do not need a tightwad or a jealous man. I don't tolerate ignorance or stupidity, and I have a short fuse for foolishness. What, God? Oh, you say that's too much?! Okay, I am open for you to fix that situation before you send him, because I retired from teaching children.

Goodness gracious, I'm going to have to repent again before I finish this letter. Forgive me, Lord! I'm okay now, so continuing I believe a good man deserves a good woman, and vice versa to complement one another. I prefer my own race, but color-coding is okay if mixed right. I like caramel, but milk chocolate and dark chocolate are my favorite. Yum, yum! Oh, sorry again! I keep slipping, but this is important, Lord. Oh yes, please let him have on decent, not dusty, shoes ... oh my goodness, this is important.

Well finally, I totally and absolutely desire a man who truly loves me for me, one who will be my friend, my lover, and my partner for life. I desire to be a soul-winner for Jesus; he should, too. God, I know that when you send him, he'll be perfect in your sight, so I digress and say "Thank you" for the fact that there is yet a way, a door for him to enter. Thank you for hope, and faith, and that you still honor prayers that sometimes get a little selfish because you know me better than I know myself.

AMEN

HYMN OF COMFORT

Savior, More Than Life to Me

(Words by Fannie J. Crosby, 1875)

Savior, more than life to me

I am clinging, clinging close to Thee;

Let Thy precious blood applied,

Keep me ever, ever near Thy side.

Every day, every hour

Let me feel Thy cleansing power;

May Thy tender love to me…

Bind me closer, closer, Lord to Thee.

WILL THE REAL CHURCH PLEASE STAND?

This is not a directive, but an inquiry.

Will the real, true, genuine, CHURCH, please get up?

There was a game show entitled, "To Tell the Truth." Many will recall that three persons stated that they all represented one true description of one of them. The other two were deceivers, liars, and presented a false description of themselves. I know, it was only TV, but when someone asks you to tell the truth, what do you do? Do you respond in truth, or do you respond in deception? Is the stance you take because you are directed to stand by man, or is your directive from God (the Holy Spirit)?

Ephesians 6:13 states:

> Stand fast therefore in the liberty wherewith Christ hath made us free and be not entangled again with the yoke of bondage ...

Christ's definition of freedom and the Isley Brothers' song entitled "It's Your Thing" have very different meanings and very different outcomes. Soldiers take an oath to defend the Constitution of the United States of America – what does your

Christian oath say that you will defend? Christians must be careful of when and why we stand, what we stand for, and if our stance aligns with the Holy Spirit or the spirit of another. Remember freedom came by the "cross," not your "boss"!

How does the church view freedom? Let us recall the Civil Rights Movement of the 50s through the 70s, and even before then, of course, there were freedom movements. Now we want more, we expect more, we should have more respect for those whose lives were willingly taken for the cost of freedom. Then there are those lives unwillingly taken so that we might be reminded of the cost to be able to stand.

Okay, remember Jesus? He died, and we should never forget the cost paid for us to be able (or be willing) to be upright, erect, and righteous. Revelation 3:11 says:

> Behold, I come quickly: hold that fast which thou hast that no man take thy crown.

A new revival may not be needed, but certainly a revival is necessary. Hearts, spirits, minds, and bodies are commanded to line up with the mission of Christ (not man). This church still stands on a foundation, on principles, on substance. It still operates by the Word and because of the Word, or it will not work, and work is essential for sustaining and remaining. Try moving a boulder on your own. You will soon give up or go get help.

People are looking for truth. People are searching for justice. People need Christ, and the first place to look for Him should be in the house, not on the porch. Stand for Jesus in all you do, and the real church will shine through.

EVERYTHING I REALLY NEEDED TO KNOW
... I should have learned in Sunday School

GOD is real, JESUS is love.

OBEY your parents and elders, DO NOT lie!

DO NOT kill; DO NOT steal.

It is okay to ADMIT you are wrong.

SAY GRACE before you eat. SMILE.

Do RIGHT and right will follow you.

DON'T do evil for evil. TURN the other cheek.

RUN NOT to trouble and AVOID mischief.

CARE for Yourself. CARE for others.

Live in GODLY FEAR. COUNT your BLESSINGS.

PRAY every day (and night).

SEEK WISDOM AND KNOWLEDGE.

SOW good seeds and APPRECIATE the weeds.

All of GOD'S creatures DESERVE good care.

Say PLEASE and THANK YOU.

KNOW your enemies. Do things DECENTLY and in ORDER.

WEAR your armor all of the time.

DRESS like QUEENS and KINGS who BELONG to CHRIST.

JUDGE not that you be not judged.

REMEMBER Jesus wept.

NEVER forget where ALL of your BLESSINGS come from,

and most of all…

GIVE THANKS, FOR THIS IS THE WILL OF GOD.

YOU ARE NOT YOUR OWN

People today will talk straight over you.

I don't know if they are trying to prove themselves or prove their intellect.

One thing is sure – speeding up your responses won't cure their practice of domineering because they are validated by their crazy notions

They can't stand for someone to have a little knowledge, whether they did or didn't go to college.

They want to know who said what, where, and when, but they forgot that misrepresentation of the Word is a sin.

Why do they offer bitter water and peculiar looks to those they claim to love? Have they even taken time to check the book? Oh, what book, they ask? The Book, the B-I-B-L-E and begin at Job 38.

This will start them going from crooked to straight.

I could ask, "Have you ever read what God said to Job when Job got a little haughty?" Well, if no, let me tell you that He spanked him with the Word, and here is what He said in Job 40: 7,8:

> Dress for action like a man; I will question you, and you make it known to me.

> "Will you even put me in the wrong? Will you condemn me that you may be in the right?

> What day was it that you turned night into day?

Rebellious children reap rebellion and dishonor – maybe not today, but there is a tomorrow. One cannot escape any chastening from above; so, on your knees with prayer, fill your heart with love, and do not forget … more people know the web you weave, the way you practice deception, or the way you come and the way you leave. Nothing is hidden from God, not my Lord! He is still sitting on the throne!

And you, you are not your own. (period)

STANDING IN THE MIDDLE
(For Gracie)

WHERE DOES ONE STAND WHEN SURROUNDED BY THE ENEMY EVEN WHEN THE ENEMY IS ME?

It may be an ancient technique or perhaps just a stance taken when one is at the crossroads looking for the next move forward. When you've come this far, and suddenly there's absolutely no movement, no action, and no voice that speaks affirmation, you feel stuck, complacent, inoperable, and even so stagnated that a push forward results in a pile-up like football players stopping a run. People get tackled by things that may seem easy for some, but others find this to be a lockdown, a place hard to move from, even when getting there was easy. It happens! What happens? Life happens, but so does death, and being in situations without God may leave you in an alone place, void of help.

The ages have taught us much, like how to honor and respect time-honored reflective moments. Remember that there was a woman accused of committing adultery in John 7. She was in the middle of accusers who vowed to kill her for actions they believed deserving of her death. How was she to escape being surrounded by these overwhelming forces? Were these accusers angry at her, or guilty themselves for knowing her? She may have even whispered a prayer asking, "Where is my exodus, where is my help?" Then came Jesus amid them, to speak on her behalf.

Now, raise your hands if you've ever been in the middle, in a place of circumstances unfavorable for you, cast into a "no exit" situation, a place where you feel s-t-u-c-k! The world and all its cares surround you, and you decide to either find a breakthrough or succumb (yield). Don't falter, don't die here...this is not the time to give over. God will provide a way of escape, but you must do your part.

- Plan times for self-affirmations. Resist the devil and he will flee! Use Daniel's prayer plan and the faith of the Hebrew boys. Seek help in the medical profession, because God gives them wisdom too!
- Go out on a limb ... Peter asked Jesus to allow him to come out on the water, and, when he kept his eyes on Jesus, Peter was safe. You must take the first step out, especially if it means from darkness to light.

- Trust God and trust yourself. Challenge yourself to make your calling and election sure. Know who you belong to and claim your royal status. In other words, learn to reign with Him because of Him! Find your personal strength and power for existence.

- Know that people have no real estate claims in heaven or hell except what bears their name, and the property in heaven may wear an eviction sign. It's okay to work here and retire in a better place (see Philippians 3:14-15).

- One more thing, REJOICE in your suffering (AMEN) which produces endurance. Endurance produces character which produces hope, and hope does not put us to shame because God's love has been poured into our hearts through the Holy Spirit who has been given to us (see Romans 3:5).

Many of us are in the middle of our breakthrough, breakout, or just a break that releases us from sorrow to satisfaction; and from awful to awesome. Athletes have a great tool called stretching – a technique designed to loosen and lubricate muscles for endurance. When you stretch out in Christ, you will have endurance for this human race. You will become stronger with every game plan, and remember...

Stay on the Lord's side, the winning side. The middle is all a test to help you reach your best, for God can do anything but fail, so fight on like a good soldier. Then know that your reward (your moment of truth) awaits you!

MY BODY, MY BODY, MY SOUL

If change is dependent upon evolution, will change not come again?

My body belongs to God – period!

Genesis 1: 27 says:

> So God created man he created him in his own image ,
> in the image of God created he him; male and female
> created he them.

The quote above simply suggests that with each generation there is an excuse or new definition for "change." Unfortunately, people are not the keepers of time or evolution and its reference or effect on the same, so essentially what evolves once will evolve again.

Consider this matter grounds for accepting the fact that, yes, my body belongs to God and so does my soul! The God who I serve is eternal, immortal, and invisible. He is wise and the King of all nations. I was created to be like Him, but not be Him ... hmm, this is where Satan messed up. To be like Jesus is to display the character of Him in this mortal body until there is eternal change.

Still, my body belongs to God. I yield the same to him. You may or may not agree, but this might be personal for the true believer. You can choose and if you disagree, pray for me and I'll pray for thee. These things, i.e., piercings, tattoo markings, etc., are not of God. The personal need to decorate the body is an offense discussed in the Old Testament book of Leviticus, and some say, "That was then, this is now." They add that we are no longer under the law, but we are subject to grace.

This calls for a review of the Word. Grace is God's unmerited favor (no more/no less). Jesus told us that He came not to destroy the law but to fulfill it. Leviticus is a book of law, so Jesus confirms His support of the law (see Matthew 5:17-20). Simple deduction, right? We all have real estate for two homes, the one of earthly clay, and the one our soul is housed in while living in the earthly one. I must pay to reside in both. I pay with man's currency for the earthly home; I pay restitution through holy and faithful living for the other.

One may decide to sell, rent, or lease the earthly home, even the soul within. Do we barter with our bodies when it comes to heavenly existence? Many carefully devote daily care toward the wear and tear of these bodies, but also put anything in or on them. I'm not going to dwell here, well, why not? So, let's see what Galatians 5:17 states.

> For the flesh desires what is contrary to the Spirit, and the Spirit what is contrary to the flesh. They are in conflict with each other, so that you are not to do whatever you want.

Practical Exercise

- Now go back and circle the words "sacrifice" and "holy."
- Research what God means when He says, "Be ye holy, for I am holy."
- Ask someone whether they believe that you are a representative of holiness.
- Go back and revisit the statement that we are made in His image, then change any answer you need to change.

Your body and your soul are not things to play with. It truly is a matter of life or death and one or the other will be your plight from moment to moment. Some might say, "But I can choose both ..."

What? Hush Your Mouth! What Did You Say?

Here is a formula: x = the beginning of eternal life. Find for "x". Okay, who am I fooling when I don't do algebra, but I do know a little Bible wisdom. It was at the cross that we were given the right to the Tree of Life. This is the same tree we encounter from the Garden of Eden. (Adam and Eve are probably having a flashback moment). This right to life is not mortal life, but eternal life with Christ where one can live forever.

There is a condition for this to occur – you must experience the death of your sins. There must be an epitaph for selfish, ungodly, worldly, unholy thoughts and reactions. In order to lose chains that bind and unlock treasures here on earth, repentance is an answer to "x". Many things can kill the body, but sin is a weapon of destruction, so repentance came by the Jesus's experience at the cross, and the method still works.

> "For the wages of sin is death; but the gift of God is eternal life through Jesus Christ our Lord." (Romans 6:23)

In order to live and reign with Him, in order to occupy that mansion in the sky, there is a price to pay – you must die!

One more thing since you're going to die anyway, you might as well die to live again. Consider that every day with Jesus is sweeter than the day before. Living with Jesus means that you have favor in unfavorable times. It means that you can call Him anytime and he'll answer. The Holy Spirit will rest, rule, and abide with you, and he'll give you good measure shaken together and running over.

SOMEONE SHOULD SAY – HALLELUJAH, ANYHOW!

BOUNDARIES, TRADITIONS, AND THE WORD

"Resilience is an asset for continuing the mission of our forefathers in the gospel."

If you draw a line or circle around yourself, can you commit yourself to the safe space where you stand? Will you ever know what is on the other side of the boundary? Let's be honest. This is an attempt to change the narrative from the word "tradition" to the word "boundaries." In certain venues (mostly the church), it seems there is a nuance for finding an excuse to avoid following patterns of experience that keep us whole. There are phrases such as "that's how they used to do it"; or "this is (insert any year), not 1900, and things have changed." Admittedly there are a lot of changes in this world, but to be honest, all change is not prosperous.

The public school system lost ground years ago over the controversial case over prayer in school. One woman caused the difference in keeping children and school personnel safe all day to children and personnel not knowing if they will return safely home. Prayer Is a good tradition and one worth keeping. Now surely because of the number of bilingual children here in the U.S., some change of acceptance could be rendered, but it does not mean that prayer is old and outdated. As for me and my house, we will pray! Should there be boundaries for when and where? Maybe. Should there be standards in place that allow all who choose to pray to do so privately or collectively? Certainly.

This nation was founded on principles, not tradition, and those principles have been revised over and over. The church was founded on a rock, a solid rock, that cannot be shaken or moved, yet there are those who want to revise it, mix it up a little, make it their own. To those persons, please know that you are treading in dangerous waters. Jesus told Peter who the builder and the maker is.

God did not spend six days working on all this heaven and earth for some human(s) to come along and erase it, but the enemy is always aware of easy targets, always aware of simple-mindedness and of those who really slip and slide in and out of truths.

God is so infinite and full of wisdom that He alone can see all, be everywhere at one time, and know every thought you have before you think it. When He said, "I am the way, the truth, and the light," who was He talking to? When He declared that "heaven and earth shall pass away but my words shall not pass away," who was He talking to? When He said, "I am God all by myself," who was He talking to? The point is that nothing in the Word has changed – just the people who would say that He wasn't talking to them.

There can be misunderstanding of the Word or misinformation of the same, and that happens a lot, but consider your options. Every believer is admonished to get an understanding of the Word. Pray and convene with God to see what He is really saying. Try the spirit by the Spirit and leave no stone unturned.

The traditional church might be described as one that still opens service with the deacons reading from the King James version and praying leftover prayers, the choir swings (oh sorry) marches in, the offering baskets pass down the pew (hopefully all the cash makes it to the end), announcements are rendered by some saint with boobs, and the preacher wears a drab color to preach everybody into heaven.

The next week they all come back and do it all over again. The nontraditional church may have a praise team open the service, deacons pray and read scripture on the phone (because they can't locate Hosea in the Bible); announcements are posted onscreen; offerings are taken online; and the preacher has on dungarees. How is that for tradition without boundaries? Which scenario will win over heaven?

Neither one!

Here's a thought: Read Romans 8:35-37 which reads:

> There is therefore now no condemnation to then which are in Christ Jesus, who walk not after the flesh, but after the Spirit, for the law of the Spirit of Life in Christ Jesus hath made me free from the law of sin and death. For what the law could not do, in that it was weak through the flesh, God sending his own Son in the likeness of sinful flesh, and for sin, condemned sin in the flesh.

Folks, it's the Word (word) that saves; it is sin drama that kills. In fact, the less dramatic church is, the more you will hear the Word. The less dramatic those in leadership appear, the more you hear the Word. Less mess, less flesh, more Word (word)! Now ask yourself, what church will allow you to hear the Gospel truth?

Begin with the end in mind. If eternal life, a mansion for living quarters, and seeing Jesus every day is your goal, then fight for it! He (Jesus) hears a lot of people calling His name, but He doesn't necessarily know them the way you want Him to know you. Trust His Word each day, and keep the good that was planted in you.

ONWARD AND UPWARD

Well, it seems you're on your way to a better day, but before you get so happy, let's talk about serving a just God. Our God is justified in all He does. Why? Because He is God, and He is our best advocate, as well as serving as judge and jury. He is Judge Advocate General, and yet he's not able to always find us deserving of the things we desire. He did say that He will supply all our needs according to His riches in glory. It is good to serve a rich God. Everything in heaven and in earth belongs to him. Yes, my Daddy is loaded – Ching, Ching!

Now brace yourself, this just in, God never said you'll not suffer while in this earthly body. He has never said that heartaches, disappointment, disaster, famine, and death wouldn't plague us.

What He *has* said is that he'll never leave us nor forsake us. Whatever we go through, He is right there. When troubles and trials surface, He can provide an elixir, that balm in Gilead. Trust that He is so wise that He knows in advance of any troubles or struggles. My God's wisdom is unmatched and not prejudiced or one-sided. This God is an AMAZING GOD! I love Him and this battle to help you understand your course is personal to me ... so,

STOP

LOOK

LISTEN

and better yet, YIELD not to temptation so that He can move us forward. Forward is a directive, not a direction (or you decide). Philippians 3:141 tells us to press toward the mark for the prize of the high calling of God in Christ Jesus.

We have all committed a crime against God, and it's time to own it. Our perfect selves have been vulnerable to the enemy in us, and the failure button was pushed. None of us escapes the trials and temptations of the enemy who told us he'd be back. He tried to come up with something different to pursue us with but has kept repeating the same three crazies on each approach.

Why do we intentionally set ourselves up to be killed daily, thought of as nothing, and regarded as dung! There is One who loves and has proven this love repeatedly. Is the test too hard?

What test, you ask? The test after the commitment to serve all the days of your life, that test!

Pause for a moment and think about your yesterday versus your today. Would you trade it? Why or why not? Dwelling on yesterday solves nothing and nothing is gained. Do you know anyone who can be your "Push Coach"? Do you know anyone who can help you thresh at the threshing floor? Hold on, here's the question: Do you know anyone who is willing to go to hell and plead your case for you? Oops! Remember Jonah? Those on the boat with him were not willing to perish for him, so Jonah had to get thrown off the boat, get swallowed up, and be held captive for three days and nights before finally getting where he was supposed to be in the first place. Stop digressing and get where you are supposed to be.

Onward and upward is a call requiring movement. Say Amen! Now rejoice and be glad that you are acquainted with a Savior who is His own chauffeur. Oh, I know, ask God to be your "Push Coach," your ride or die. When it comes to getting the fix you need, He is a fixer. When it comes to needing medication, He is the physician to call. When you get down to the "I don't have it," He is your provider. The songwriter Charles Price Jones (born 1865) penned these words :

Jesus Christ is made to me,

All I need, all I need

He alone is all my plea

He is all I need."

YOUR NET WORTH

In the game of life, there are no substitutes for your life. You get one life to live. You have one life to prove yourself worthy of personal accomplishments, successes, and yes, failures. What is your measuring apparatus for your life? Is it based on what the average eye can't see? Is it perhaps written in a book or movie, or just sung loudly by those who love you? Is it measured by temperature or treasures? Is the Savior counted into your equation?

Would you rather your worth be evaluated by a relative or a friend? Do you trust an enemy more than a frenemy? Job had friends who questioned the deeds he did that may have led to his losses. They knew him well enough to ask him, but did they know him well enough to not accuse him? When someone falls, why attach a boulder to their neck? Saul's son Jonathan knew David as a friend, a trustworthy friend, so was Jonathan obligated to show him compassion in a situation influenced by his family's position or was Jonathan expecting something because he saw David's pending worth?

What is your worth? This is usually assigned to define the value of a business, but it can prove applicable here, so again, what is your net worth?

This should be an easy response. Someone named Jesus took the time, the pain, and the journey of thirty-three years that resulted in one CROSS experience. This one event has given you the credentials to be called worthy. It is His net worth that produced and produces the value of each life and the right to eventually reign with him. His worth is not dependent upon your worth. You are on your own to prove that what Christ did for you is not in vain.

So, are you worthy? Is your "all" on the altar bowed as a sacrificial lamb or is this not important to you?

The rich and famous respond with money, but that is just stubble, and it does not make them worthy (or wealthy). Athletes may say their years in the sports arena contribute much and make them worthy. Physicians and attorneys, judges and teachers, even preachers may consider that their call to service is worth much. After all, none of these would turn down a financial increase for a task so honorable. The Bible shares that it is the Lord who is worthy, good, moral, and upright, holding to honesty and respectable living. Can you compete with that? Should you try? Yesssssssssssssssss, if by God's lead, by all means necessary mimic His worth!

The Lord (the worthy Lamb) is searching for a church (you) without spot or wrinkle or any such thing. He is looking for your reflection of Him that mimics His journey including the "cross" (not literally). You have probably found yourself in many positions and situations where you ask, "Is this real," or "Am I dreaming?"– hopeful of waking before calamity strikes. You may call out "Jesus!" S.O.S., or a spoken cry for 911. Oh, yea whatever ill words you are thinking should be returned to the pit before speaking....

What is important is that you have chosen to and desire to look like Jesus, to walk and talk like Jesus, to mimic His work but fear Him you must, for fear is the beginning of wisdom – so be afraid. You don't have to be Job, but you do have to face your challenges head on. You do not have to sin like David, but you must learn the dance of righteousness step by step. Fear brings an understanding of worth, so greet it like a friend knowing that your best friend Jesus is not a substitute but the real thing, the real worthy one – so worthy.

Your net worth is predicated on good deeds, deeds that honor God's glory, not for praise to you. The Holy Spirit is designed to boost the Godhead, not you. The opportunity to show others the God in you is an opportunity to allow Him to shine through you. Remember that Isaiah 64:6 reads:

> But we are all as an unclean thing, and all our righteousness are as filthy rags; and we all do fade as a leaf; and our iniquities, like the wind, have taken us away.

In other words our works mean nothing if we get the glory or the praise, because it will dissolve as nothing. On the other hand, when God receives our offer we will rejoice, for greater is He that is in us, than he who chooses the world!

What is your net worth, and is it enough for the purchase of a home in glory?

IT IS ABOUT ME
(DOCUMENTING TRUTH)

With the rest of the Old Testament prophecies of the Messiah in mind, and in light of the New Testament accounts of Jesus fulfilling all those prophecies, it is clear that God's promise to Adam and Eve in Genesis 3:15 was the first promise of the Savior.

If we need any more proof that Genesis 3:15 speaks of the first Gospel promise, all we need do is look at Satan's actions after that promise was given. Satan was engaged in a relentless but futile effort to destroy the ancestral line of the Messiah and then to kill the Christ child himself. Satan understood what God's promise in Genesis 3:15 was all about.

> And I will put enmity
>
> Between thee and the woman,
>
> And between thy seed and her seed;
>
> It shall bruise thy head, and thou shalt bruise his heel.

How thankful we can be that God gave sinners one promise after another of a Savior.

And then, in Galatians 4:4-5, we read:

> "But when the fulness of time was come, God sent
> forth his Son, made of a woman, made under the law, to
> redeem them that were under the law, that we might
> receive the adoption of sons."

I Understand Better Today What I Did Not Understand Yesterday

That is a monumental statement for me to make. In studying God's Word and listening to the Word as I study, I asked an all-important question: Lord, when did it begin that you decided to send us a savior? Genesis 3:15 is the response He showed to me, and yes, it took a moment to digest why His words suggested that the answer is Jesus. But keep reading as I did, because I've come to realize that this is about ME! You also have the privilege to say that this is also about YOU!

Have you ever watched a situation grow from good to evil? Have you ever observed a person being attacked by the enemy and the enemy is so confident that they are winning that they start talking trash? In the recording for Genesis 3:15 God has had enough of this opposition from Lucifer's new form. He tells this serpent exactly what He will do to keep him away from His own people, and He inevitably states what will be done to prevent the approach of sin and the destruction of His own. God warns Satan and makes good on His warning (his promise) in Jeremiah, Isaiah. And other major and minor prophets as well as in the Gospels.

Yesteryear my mind was on Christ, just not in Christ. I knew better but chose the opposite. So when I reflected upon all of the Sunday School, Revivals, and sermons over the years, I began to see a better way, a better motivation for service.

See, I told you that this is about me, and you can say that it is about you! Every word that proceeds out of the mouth of God is about us, collectively as His own. He has committed this gospel, this dispensation, the Word so that every chapter and verse written is intended for M-E, me!

It is imperative that at some juncture we stop giving the enemy cause to control our destiny by using catch phrases like "It ain't about YOU"! Affirm the principle of self-preservation, stand, and declare that it is indeed about you! God has said, in Isaiah 46:9-10:

> Remember the former things of old: for I am God, and there is none like me, Declaring the end from the

beginning, and from ancient times the things that are not yet done, saying, My counsel shall stand, and I will do all my pleasure.

The entire 66 books of the Bible are about me (and you), and the sooner we claim what is, the sooner we can be about our Father's business. You know the phrase, "If you don't stand for something, you'll fall for anything." The commercials, catch phrases, jingles, etc. that are constantly poured into our Spirit by the opposition is detrimental to our progress and the building or rebuilding of our confidence in Christ Jesus. The question is, who do you believe?

Here's another misnomer you've heard and received: "You can wear anything to church that you desire." Major infraction, and you're being set up to be messed up. Matthew 11:28 gives the "come as you are theory" stating:

Come unto me, all ye that labour and are heavy laden, and I will give you rest.

And all the people who work hard and are burdened with a lot of duties, make your way toward Jesus, and He will provide you with leisure from the drudgery of everyday life. Okay, now is a good time to play hide-and-seek. Where in this passage does the Lord mention clothing? Nowhere! The passage refers to the human spirit's condition of hunger and thirst for the Word.

I don't know who started the idea that "come as you are" references clothing, but it doesn't. However, there is a standard for how to attire your flesh when you are a follower of Christ. First remember that clothing serves (among other things) for covering your flesh, beauty for your enjoyment, and uniformity for your profession. Now, which of these do you think Christ is concerned with? Why did you select that answer?

Although God is Spirit and cannot be seen as flesh, He sent His son Jesus to be clothed in righteousness when represented by those in the flesh, to wear the garment of praise, and to model for us the character of God. It is our flesh, our choice, and our rebellion that changes the essence of how we present ourselves before Christ. Remember Romans 12:1 in a previous passage. Covering yourself and being clothed in righteousness is a safe way to please God. Remember when Adam and Eve knew they were naked, they hid. They were not so bold as to say that their found state of sin was okay, because it wasn't.

There are many who turn and twist this to serve themselves by their will and not the will of God. STOP IT, PLEASE! When it is understood that God is the Judge among judges, perhaps we will realize His standards ...

- God is a jealous God .... put nothing before him especially your flesh. (Read Galatians 5:19.)
- God said that He will know us by the fruit we bear ... good fruit yields a good harvest. (Study Galatians 5: 22-23.)
- "God is not mocked; whatsoever a man soweth, that shall he also reap." (Galatians 6:7) If you do (sow weeds), you should expect God to meet you on the threshing floor as Himself. This is not a threat, but a promise.
- "Marvel not that I said unto thee, Ye must be born again." (John 3:7)
- Be very careful, then, how you live – not as unwise but as wise. (See Ephesians 5:15) The world has everything for the unrighteous, and nothing for the righteous.
- Flesh shall pass away; only what is done for Christ shall last. The ability to spiritually see (having vision), to spiritually discern (having wisdom), to faithfully execute (walk with God) has nothing to

do with your flesh except to make sure it does not get in your way.

I am not a fan of hell, and I refuse to go there. I need to keep a close watch on the desires of my flesh to be seen, my female essence to be flaunted, or my belief that the latest fashion wasn't made with me in mind, so I can rely on just my imagination (which I am also accountable for). When the unknowing tell you that you look fine, consider the mirror test...trust it for the truth!

You have a right to debate, disagree, and keep it moving, but remember this thought: If you are in leadership, if you stand before the people to minister, if you dress to please yourself without regard for who you represent, you are of the flesh, not the Spirit. In 2 Corinthians 10:3-5, Paul says:

> For though we walk in the flesh, we do not war after the flesh; (For the weapons of our warfare are not carnal, but mighty through God to the pulling down of strong holds); Casting down imaginations, and every high thing that exalteth itself against the knowledge of God, and bringing into captivity every thought to the obedience of Christ.

Everything we display should be of Spirit, not of flesh. We represent the Kingdom of God at all costs, and our fleshly ways are considered as dung.

Believers can depend on supporting the cause of the cross to change us from sinful samples to Spiritual examples, to a Jesus look-alike. So, how do you look? Who do you favor? Who is your Daddy? Whatever your answer is, don't lose sight of the fact that everything Christ did, He did it for you, He made it about you because He wants to save you. Believe this thought: There's no time like the present to begin letting the Kingdom of God know that because Christ thought enough to die for you, you are willing to follow him. What will you crucify for him?

NEBUCHADNEZZAR: A SHORT SYNOPSIS

There are offenses in the law of this land that are chargeable offenses as defined in our nation's Constitution and by-laws, and also within state and local government. There are crimes of action with intent and those that are unintentional; however, the weight of and the level of that offense is punishable by law.

Those responsible for upholding the law are often the offenders of the same, yet they go unpunished based on the unwritten law. Let us note that all who are sworn to uphold the law are not those who breech the same. However, in recent years and through recent events our eyes have been opened to see those who refuse to follow the oath they have taken. It is the same way (unfortunately) in the house of God. One bad apple can spoil the entire bunch, but our just God is fully aware and has remnants in place. Remember He told one prophet that He had plenty of soldiers, and he was not the only one?

We will examine in this play the story of King Nebuchadnezzar, Daniel, and the three Hebrew boys. You should be familiar with the facts for how this all begins, and how it ends. There were offenses committed based on who ruled the law of the land, but God said, "Well, maybe not!"

Stay tuned for the short version.

Narrator: Nebuchadnezzar seized Jerusalem and brought many captives back to Babylon. One day he decided to seek (among those taken) youths of good appearance, wise, and without blemish to be used in the King's palace. He eventually brought four that fit the description, named Daniel (Belteshazzar), Hananiah (Shadrach), Mishael (Meshach), and Azariah (Abednego) of the tribe of Judah. As time passed, one night the King had a dream ... but no one could interpret the dream until Daniel sought his God, and the dream was revealed. Daniel in fact had to interpret two dreams for this King, as will be revealed.

Note: The next passages are a rendition of the actual event contained in the book of Daniel, Chapters 3 and 4. The wording is changed to fit today's readers; the message has not changed.

Narrator: Nebuchadnezzar spoke before his court when one courts man suggested that because he was the King, he should decree that anyone who does not bow in honor of the King when the instruments play should be tossed into the fire. That sounded like a great idea to the King and so it became the mandate, and the courts man shouted the decree out loud for the entire Kingdom to hear. They wanted anybody, from wherever they came from, to deny their God and serve this god called Nebuchadnezzar. If anyone said anything against this god, or went against whatever he decreed, punishment would be the result.

(There was however a trick, a set-up, a motive.)

The courts man knew that the King had found favor with the Hebrews and on top of that, he had elevated them, especially Daniel, to a higher status than some of his own people. Jealousy is a terrible motivator and can cost you your life.

Note: When jealously prevails, nothing stops it but Christ. These men had been challenged before when it came to the eating of food that the King ordered for nourishment. They said, "No, we will only eat plant-based foods that they were accustomed to eating." The challenge was that if they maintained stature and health with their food, the King would leave the matter alone. In a few days, the King noted that they in fact were leaner and stronger from eating plant-based foods than his own people eating their customary diet.

So, the King ordered the instruments to play, and the people bowed ... well almost all of them. It was reported that Daniel and the Hebrew boys did not bow. So, the King ordered the playing of instruments again, and again they did not bow. Of course (this likely pleased the courtsman, thinking he would finally get rid of these three), King Nebuchadnezzar ordered that Shadrach, Meshach, and Abednego be thrown into the furnace and that it be turned up in temperature seven times its usual level.

Note: Someone should say here that serving the Lord will pay off not just after a while, but right now. Some of us have furnace situations every day. Some of us are challenged each day to serve an idol god, a false god. When you have people with you of the same mind as Christ, things work out for your good. Somebody should be willing to stand up for Jesus!

Nebuchadnezzar and all the people important to him watched as the boys were thrown in. Those obeying the King and who complied to this matter were consumed by the fire while throwing the boys in.

Something else was occurring as they watched and awaited the outcome. The King asked, "Did we not throw three in the fire, but behold, I see four and one looks like the Son of God." Surely this was impossible, but when the doors were opened, all three boys walked out without a smoke smell, and without being seared.

Nebuchadnezzar responded, "Blessed be the God of Shadrach, Meshach, and Abednego who has sent His angel and delivered His servants, who trusted in Him, and set aside the king's command, and yielded up their bodies rather than serve and worship any god except their own God." Then he added that there be a new decree that if anyone spoke against the God of these three, "they shall be torn limb from limb, and their houses laid in ruins, for there is no other god who is able to rescue in this way."

Note: It is when you prove whose you are that promotion comes. One should never be concerned or worried about a man or woman promoting you to higher office unless God is in the plan. If God has gotten in your furnace with you and delivered you, say Amen!

Oh, did you ask: What about Daniel?

Daniel had this regimen where he prayed three times a day, and he wasn't quiet about it. He would hoist up his window and pray so that whosoever would hear him did hear him. Daniel's prayers were nonsense to others, and they convinced the King to charge him with an offense. Daniel was thrown into the den of lions, but he laid down and got up without being attacked, without a scar, and without shame.

King Nebuchadnezzar's continued actions against these men of God gave him this chargeable offense. His blatant response to hearing and disobeying, choosing idols for worship, and disregard of the Hebrew God created years of punishment and disbarring from the throne. This King looked and acted like a natural animal in a habitat not of his choosing.

God's wrath is nothing to play with. When provoked He has the authority to correct and the authority to restore. Faith could have saved Nebuchadnezzar, but he chose not to be faithful. Love could have saved him, but he chose not to exercise loving ways. He was the King, and that seemingly was enough for him to have what he wanted. Think again!

The grace of God is a gift not to be readily forgotten. His mercy and grace are extended to us all, but it is not to be taken for granted. It is not to be abused, flaunted, thwarted, or used as a weapon. Is God blind or deaf? Does He sleep or show a lack of wisdom? Has He lost or sold any part of His throne such that a "For Lease" sign is posted. Absolutely not! Who dares to challenge this Lord of lords, this King of kings, this Alpha and

Omega? Whose house (Kingdom) is this? God allows dominion over His creation just as He did with Adam and Eve, but who can forget that story?

When God shared with Peter that upon this rock, He would build His church, He meant exactly that. This likely established the first real estate event. Perhaps we should all check our personal deed of ownership to see if we still reside on that Rock. Does this body and mind officially live in Christ? Our physical buildings where we worship may be a conflict for true service, especially when we forget that God is seeking honor from your own tabernacle with the whole of you, from the outside in and inside out.

Too many people flaunt God thinking that (like Nebuchadnezzar), they can get away with anything they want. Leaders, parents, and other authorities are allowing too many idols to dictate and disrupt God's original plans. We are just as indebted to God now as our forefathers were from the beginning, and the debt increases. Who shall be able to pay? Our many offenses create a greater cost with each sin and with each disobedient notion.

Daniel and the Hebrew boys stayed faithful to the God of Abraham, Isaac, and Jacob. Who are you faithful to? Whose side are you leaning on? Where is your refuge? What name do you call your God? Here is a hint … call Him Savior, Lord, Everlasting Father, Creator of this world, Mighty God, and you may continue this and fight out loud like Daniel!

Jesus is on the main line, call Him up and tell Him what you want. He will open the windows of Heaven and pour, pour, pour for when he reigns in your life and praises go forth you receive joys unspeakable. Faithfulness yields gifts from above. Disobedience yields the opposite!

PHYSICIAN, HEAL THYSELF

I choose to make this section personal, and I am not ever willing to do so, yet it is important. In Luke 4:23 Jesus speaks in response to people's complaints about His healing everywhere but where they want Him to heal. Then there is the idea that rather than focusing on someone else's behavior or choices; focus on your own. Hmm! Reflection is a wonderful and necessary process, but once completed and corrections (if needed} are made ... then what?

This cannot be a one-sided matter as some behold the issue of racism. It's not the racist who is at fault, they might declare – it's the person of color who has the problem. It's not the thief or the attacker who is at fault, they might insist – it's the person who was attacked and provoked it. It wasn't Emmett Till's imperfect speech that allegedly got him in trouble – it was the fact that his mom sent him away for the summer without teaching him phonics. (Right!}

Is this ridiculous enough for you? Which account do you believe? Do you even consider how many different scenarios people come up with to justify their mistakes, shortcomings, or even their ignorance? What's the real excuse? There's always an excuse and then there is the absolute truth!

These days it is hard to separate facts from fiction, yet there is always TRUTH. My personal truth is simple, watch for the "I support Jesus' look" or the "I support evil" look. It helps if you're a parent and you've developed a discernment for the truth versus a lie in your child's face. It also helps if you can remember your own efforts to distort real events from unreal or partially true matters. Either way, one is right, and one is wrong!

Have you ever thought that you'd make a good judge or attorney or physician? Decisions are made based on the information presented. Notice I didn't say the "facts" presented. Most people don't want to know how to prevent cancer. They just want to know how to get rid of it if they get it. Offenders don't care about the damage caused because of their offense, just how to get away with it. I remember hearing my students use the phrase "I don't care," and yes, I've said it a time or two myself, but care is what Jesus had for us when He hung on the cross.

Don't forget that He was there for a crime He didn't commit, yet people use this story as an excuse to say it's okay if you face the same challenge. IT'S NOT OKAY!!! The truth is that He died there so that we wouldn't have to repeat the nonsense. He died there for the sake of preventing false trials, He died there to offer light versus the dark. How many more people will DIE because of evil designs?

Oh, let me not forget to talk about the cowards out there who see it and say nothing, do nothing, and certainly do not help rectify wrong. Cowards are people who love to ride the train that looks like it's headed for personal satisfaction. They ride, relax, and become complacent, regardless of the fact that people are murdered (James 3:6) on the train, slander occurs on the train, double-minded people ride the train, people who lack the "fruit of the spirit" ride the train – all engaged in the same sin of theft and destruction.

Don't be deceived, there are good people onboard too, and they see, hear, and absorb everything going on, but remain silent. SAD, SAD, and pitiful – how we want justice but will not participate in it. We want justice, as long as its existence doesn't depend on us!

People seem to like justice when it is on option for saving their own rear part. Oh yeah, Justice is a nice name for a boy, but where is "justice" when there is contempt, harshness, compliance, and complacency? Who among you can issue the justification act that supports light? Is it you? Are you sure? Why or why not? Is it easy is it for you to see injustice and let it ride, knowing there is a disservice when turning blind eye or deaf ear?

Do you rest comfortably knowing the wrong is wrong, and do you go soundly to sleep without even a prayer of cleansing? What's wrong with us? Allow me to identify the "us," but you know exactly who I mean – Unleavened Saints ... the ones who quote 2 Chronicles 7:14 (like it's a drink of water):

> If my people, who are called by my name, shall humble themselves, and pray, and seek my face, and turn from their wicked ways; then will I hear from heaven, and will forgive their sin, and will heal their land.

Pleas-s-s-e STOP! Again, double-minded, unleavened workers of iniquity – STOP!

Learn to stand for what is right. It's time to be bold against the evil that so easily besets us. STOP accepting just any explanation for the sake of friendship, kinship, and remember the prophet Jonah. Don't be thrown off the ship.

STOP SIGN GOSPEL

STAND UP FOR CHRIST

FIGHT LIKE DAVID FOUGHT

SHUN EVIL

PREY LESS

PRAY MORE

PROTECT YOUR EARS

PROTECT YOUR EYES

VALUE YOUR SOUL

Romans 12:9 says:

> ABHOR that which is evil, cleave to that which is good. Everything about the Word is good. Hold fast to him that can save your soul, and who can present you faultless before the Father which is in Heaven. Hold to him that sees and knows all light and dark; the one true Judge and jury of all who will stand before him.

And remember Ephesians 6:11:

Put on the whole armor of God that ye may be able to stand against the wiles of the devil.

Finally, think about Timothy 1:17:

Now unto the King eternal, immortal, invisible; the only wise God, be honor and glory forever. Amen

HOMECOMING

If you are peeping through the kitchen window on a Saturday evening and the pots and pans are in full steam, it must be time for another Homecoming Sunday in the Tennessee countryside. Kitchen shuffling didn't just happen at my house, but in the homes of many who were anxiously awaiting this annual date, this great day of gathering since the winter yielded spring.

It was customary or traditional that churches set aside a Sunday for those born and raised, those who left the small area for larger ground, neighbors, and visiting church friends to come and celebrate another year of service in the Kingdom. It was also a time to build finances for the church to either pay last winter's bills or to save for the next.

Homecomings always brought out our Sunday best. Men in common-colored suits and ties, or overalls nicely starched, pressed, and cuffed. Women in cat eyeglasses or maybe wire-rimmed, wearing belted dresses. Girls in prissy socks and can-can dresses so wide it took up two seats. The boys were easier to dress in just a buttoned-down shirt and suspenders holding up older brothers' last year's trousers.

It was always the first Sunday in June for the church in Sandy Hook, Tennessee where Elder Young was the Pastor. This is the church of my mother's family and my father's ministry. It had a gigantic appearance to me with steps leading to the one-room sanctuary that held about 75 people. The unisex human waste deposit site was across the street down a rugged weedy path that hosted two pebble-like rock seats, no doors for privacy, and just the walls. It's no telling what lurked beneath those holes, but God protected us.

The deacons prayed fervent prayers, the congregation sang the most amazing songs of Zion, and people danced and shouted Hallelujah out of hoisted-up windows. Two and a half hours later no one was tired or weary, just anxious to finally eat the food stored in all the coolers in the back seats of the cars parked outside ... umm-umm, good.

The year captured in the photo on the next page was 1949. The congregants included my parents and three sisters; aunts and cousins; neighbors and friends that I would eventually meet. I love this picture. Each face tells a story and even the hairstyles show strength and poise.

My mom is holding my sister born in 1948. When my brother and I were born, the tradition continued in Sandy Hook, Hohenwald, Mt. Pleasant, and even as far as Sheffield, Alabama. I even remember that when the building was no longer in use and I taught in a county close by, I'd go by to see it and reminisce about days and people I missed.

In 1983, the building, although it hadn't been used in years, was torched by youths from the community. It was a Halloween stunt that erased a standing artifact – a community pillar, a place where people turned for comfort and joy. I am grateful that most of the people in the 1949 photograph were not alive to see this tragedy, but for those who remained and remember, it was devastating. It was cruel and apparently intentional, heartless, and maybe fueled by anger of some type, but I think there is a moral to the story.

It was not just a building, but more importantly the work inside of it for all those years served as spiritual evidence that it was positively sanctified, holy, God-approved, and people-approved. The inside work in this and other sanctuaries were and are evidence of God's hand. Ask me how I know! Okay, I know because of the number of remaining congregants who testify of how they made it through the good and the bad, knowing that God is good, and were able to keep holding on until change would come. Oh yes, one more truth known to us, the remnants of that church – WE are the church. The church lives within us, stays with us, and determines our destiny, but one thing is relative and relevant – sometimes, you must go home!

POEMS

DEW DROPS

Let dew drops from heaven rain on me.
Let your breath Lord breathe on me.
Set my soul on fire and have your way in me.
Quench me with living water so that I bless thee.

Now, Lord, please shape my mouth to honor your word,
And mold my tongue that my thoughts will not be heard.
Then send dew drops from Heaven upon my head.

WAIT UNTIL TOMORROW

Do you ever feel as if this is your theme song?

Wait until tomorrow when the clouds will go away,

And be grateful for the smallest things that brighten the day!

Wait until tomorrow – it will clear up all the rain,

Or sleeping on it shall create sunshine out of pain.

Oh, how about this one – count to ten and take it in stride.

Consider it a blessing…it could be worse next time.

Forget the past and look ahead.

Take no hostages and no blood will be shed,

And when the morrow dawns and your windows open wide,

Remember you waited, and proceed with this in mind.

Tomorrows are made because today will no longer exist,

And the memory becomes yesterday

where your problems are mere BLISS!

CHURCH FOLK

Two eyes look upon me with hatred,
One mind thinks of me with rage.
One heart has no love for me, two hands raise to disclaim me—
Yet you lie to God and say you love me.

You nail me upon approach, fake a smile and wish for a rope.
Yes, you'd hang me without a second thought…
Then you lie to God and say you love me.

Your game is exposed, no shame do you show.
You've done this for so long that it's a part of your make-up…
You smile and tell God you love me.

With two feet you trod upon me and with one tongue
you slay me.
From your belly you spit me out then offer me a cup…
Once again you lie and tell God you love me.

Well, I love you and this is true. Stab me, hate me, shame me,
curse and abuse me.
Well, why not crucify me? Oh, that's what they did to Jesus,
but guess what?
I do love you, and God knows this too…
But you will lie and say this is not about YOU!

SEEDLING

Once I was a seed with really no place to go…
Until someone planted me,
Now I can grow!

I AM

I am not afraid of the dark for Jesus is the light.
I am not afraid to speak praise for my battle he will fight.
I am a child of the most-high God and his son
sitting on his right.
I am just a child and Jesus Christ is in control of my night!

MANY THANKS

No one begins or goes through life without help or assistance
to become better. Here are a few of those who have made my
days better and to whom I could openly say ... THANK YOU!

I truly thank my parents Elder Monzell and Sister Roberta
(Crowley) McFarland for raising me in love for, and fear of,
God. I also had great maternal and paternal grandparents, aunts
and uncles, siblings, and then there are my children and grands.
I love and cherish you all. This understanding of the Word of
God probably has taken (for me) longer than God intended. But
I am grateful that He has given me grace and mercy to redeem
myself.

I want to also thank many pastors and ministers of the Original
Church of God who have preached and taught this gospel in
such a way that it compelled me and others to stay in the
narrow way, not with the world. I recognize former Pastors of
the Original Church of God and Evangelist Patricia Holmes
posthumously. I continue to appreciate encouragement from
Pastors Richardson, Truss, Childress, and Union; Prophetess
Hoskins; and Dr. Carletta J. Harlan.

I am grateful for the Believers in Christ Ministry Training that fueled my faith, a few wonderful friends that listened to me defend Christ, and I am thankful for this opportunity to just speak as Christ has spoken to me.

Thank you all and I pray that the contents of this book be not indifferent to God's Word, but support and confirm that He lives in me.

ABOUT THE AUTHOR

The author is Minister Janet M. Merriwether of Nashville,
Tennessee in Davidson County. Janet grew in knowledge while
attending public schools in Nashville and furthered her
education at the Tennessee State University with a teaching
degree and certification.

Her Christian experience extends from the womb to living,
learning, sitting, and training with some of the best gospel
leaders of her community. She sings, writes, teaches, and
preaches the Word of God knowing the value of living a life
for him.

"I will let nothing separate me from the love of God."
(Romans 8:35-39)

Janet is the youngest member of her family and traveled the most with her parents as her father, Elder Monzell McFarland, ministered the Word from Nashville to Columbia to Sandy Hook, Hohenwald, and beyond. She believes the cloak fell to her to serve God no matter where she is called to serve. Her writings reflect the experiences fought and proclaimed in her life in order to stay in Christ.

She accepted her call to ministry, preaching her first sermon on the first Sunday in July of 2001. That sermon was entitled "Proof of Purchase," and since that day, she has worked and is working to continue to prove her thanks for the experience of the Cross. She continues working as a defender of the Cross and praying always that no weapon formed against her shall prosper – it won't work!

The title shares testimony praise and purpose for living a life for Jesus. No turning back! You may see pain and despair, joy, and peace, but please understand the faith walk taken for this journey. There will always be affliction and trouble on every hand, but God's Word stands to remind all that He never fails. Minister Merriwether has permission to speak from God who sent her on this journey. Therefore, as referenced in Psalm 19:14, let the words of her mouth and the meditation of her heart be acceptable in the sight of the Lord, our strength, and our redeemer.

Amen!

These are my parents who caused me to grow and know Christ. This photo is from 1941, years before my birth. I am grateful for the time we had together.

Sunday morning and my Mom was elegant and poised. We called her Mother, her siblings called her Love, and others called her Sister Mac!

This was Christmas 1963, and I had a brand new doll.
I was posing in my brother's room. My mother's shoes
were stored there because the older houses had very
little closet space. I dreamed of the day when I could fill
her shoes in more ways than one. (Picture taken by my
sister's boyfriend.)